Bird-Woman

Em Strang

Bird-Woman

Shearsman Books

First published in the United Kingdom in 2016 by
Shearsman Books
50 Westons Hill Drive
Emersons Green
BRISTOL
BS16 7DF

Shearsman Books Ltd Registered Office
30–31 St. James Place, Mangotsfield, Bristol BS16 9JB
(this address not for correspondence)

www.shearsman.com

ISBN 978-1-84861-494-9

Contents

for my family, blood-related and not, human and not

chook, chook, tchink, tchink, tchink

– Blackbird

Apokatastasis

Light, a bird's nest.
A garment of woodpigeons, *ru-hoo ru ru-hoo*,
nodding off in the hems.
Waking up in a place
where great northern divers
are old throats from the other side,
where nothing any of us can speak of
seems real.

Bird-Woman

Nothing is yet in its true form —C.S. Lewis

The bird-woman is in the field in her blue dress,
small bird wrapped in a rag of cotton in her hand,
legs like twigs, throat between songs.

The sunlight is squeezing her, squeezing the field-grass
until her blue dress is a distant boat
and the field is the sea,
somewhere used to slipping boundaries.

Then two men, hands in pockets,
feet sinking into the grey-black of the road.
The sun is hot and high and they wade into the field,
lose themselves to the waist in straight, green blades.

The bird-woman is scuffing the soft, loose earth,
making a bowl for the body.
She lays the bird with its broken neck
and covers it with clover,
small red flowers, lucky leaves.

When the men capsize her
the pleats of her dress unfurl.

The ground takes their weight.

Bird-House

You won't believe me when I say
the house turned into a bird and flew away.
It was midday and the loosestrife was blowing
all the way through the fields to the burn
where I crossed over barefoot, knowing every pebble,
every slippery spot. The path takes a sharp turn
like a changed mind, and then the old stone steps,
the nettles and the gate which opens on its own.
The front door had grown in the sunlight,
had stretched and snapped into a sharp, tight beak
with nares like spy-holes looking into the hearth
of the bird. All cross-beams and timbers had turned
into thin, hollow bones, hooking the wings
and the flesh of the thing to its dreams.

Paris Hotel

There are times in life when the question of knowing if one can think differently than one thinks, and perceive differently than one sees, is absolutely necessary if one is to go on looking and reflecting at all. —Michel Foucault

When the maid   comes in with breakfast

        astonishment

  spills   over the bed

        like sunlight

        over our young flesh.

The maid   smiles

    at   the   pains   au chocolat

  and   all   the times

    she's quietly combed her hair

    are   in the room

    with us   then.

We are   trapeze artists –

    that's what

  comes   to mind

  as she   stands waiting,

unsure.

From

where I'm lying

I can see your pants   on   the

bathroom floor.

When we look at each other

the   doors   and   windows

expand,   warp

like   fairground   mirrors

and your cock   is a baguette.

After a while,

she sets down the tray –

there is jam;   there is hot tea

in spotless cups

like milky moons.

Penelope

It's true the door no longer fits the frame
and the windows are blown out.
Someone's been in and torn both our names
out of the curtains, the bedclothes, even that
stout little dresser we bought in the driving rain
that day I suddenly knew it was my fault –
that if I hadn't loved you so much (God, it was insane)
you wouldn't have left. No doubt
I learnt something valuable. Perhaps
I finally overcame the need to be near you,
to decorate the house with travel photographs and books,
that quaint framed poem you wrote one summer,
the one about the woman with small hands from Lastur in Spain,
who said the only way to make you listen was to shout.

Her Indoors

She's quieter than usual,
barely a trip-trap to the fridge,
brown hide soft as a rug,
eyes full of long-forgotten stories
that came from the hills
and returned to them.

She noses out green vegetables –
winter cabbage, chard, kale –
and tosses them into a pan,
dainty hooves like ash buds,
agile limbs that restrain themselves
between cooker, worktop, bench.

At 6 o'clock he'll be in
all antler and hill-breath,
canter tales that wind up the kids;
he'll sit himself down
with his haunches splayed
and bellow about the rut.

The Room

But someone, something's responsible for this. —Raymond Carver

It's like a Renaissance painting
only the men are naked, too.
One woman – breasts on her belly like French butter pears –
and twelve sacred men,
quickly circling in a dusky room in a northern city.

Some time later, two roe deer enter
and the room gets warmer.

A few of the men poke and shoo the animals
but soon the whole room is full of deer
and the men are standing among the herd
in the deep warm dark
and the woman is watching their shapes,
the winking of skin and eyeball in the moonlight.

Who knows what room this is.

The deer are quiet,
muzzles mapping the space.

Wolf

For D

Die Welt muß romantisiert werden. So findet man den ursprünglichen Sinn wieder. Romantisieren ist nichts, als eine qualitative Potenzierung. —Novalis

She has bent all night
in and out of the backwoods,
her bones looking for a way
through the pink flesh, the silver coat.

All night she has searched,
combing the woods, combing the winter river,
chalk stones redoubling the moon,
salmon ghosting the banks like a slip of the tongue.

Something has led her here
to the head of the glen,
the trees cutting a hole in the night,
more night on the fields than she's seen before,
the mountains hovering like hawks.

When she finally reaches the gorse
she catches her breath on its thorns,
curls herself into her sleep-shell,
her belly haunting her,
her body shedding its shade.

It's dawn when I find her,
grief-stiff, the rooks lifting and re-settling,
lifting and re-settling,
the sun beginning to burn.

The Feast

There are no more people in Yarmouk, only skeletons with yellow skin.
—Umm Hassan, Syria, 2014

There's nothing inside this morning

     but a blackbird.

He's pecking steadily into my eye-socket,

        the yellow beak's fidelity

making a clean meal of my eye's meat.

But it's OK.

     It's good to be useful.

The Miracle

We cross the western boundary,
carrying the body to the horses.
The flies test us all,
land on our eyelids like tiny black kisses.

The hearse horse is calm – God bless him –
as we harness and double-knot
in what little daylight's left.

It's a short ride but the stench is strong
and if the birds had been to eat
we could've saved ourselves the ritual,
could've let her lie.

It's at the low copse we notice it:
a strange light where the burials are.
It's blue like an ice-hole
or how we might imagine
the inside of the moon.

The horses snort.

Before we realise,
we've dismounted into the dust.

Someone takes off their hat
and we stand like birds.

The body is up and walking to the light,
arms and legs intact.

If we could speak,
words would climb out of our mouths
and doubt all over the night.

Conversation with Wisława Szymborska

I stand at your grave and speak.
The wind is up, whipping the trees
and a black line of mourners
leaves the church, the week's first
loss writing its path to the gate,
polished shoes spelling something
we all know, more or less, the weight
of stones, the need to begin
again in some dour town, the one
where the clock-tower chimes the hour,
hands mark the minutes one after the other
until a quarry truck comes, a megaton
of slate crashing into the street,
its layers split open, broken at our feet.

Fossil

I am a slate human,
a shining layer flaking.
If this is my time, I'll open:
twinkling mica
like small fish in a flood of black.
Do you know me?

I go down this tight river.
I'm used to being cheek by jowl,
body little in the water
as though nothing could be better.

Tight fins, breathing the brown in
and out without lungs,
silt sticking to me like love
to a clogged aorta there's so much.
I used to be other.
Do you know me?

Getting Ready to Dance

for B

The way a door swings silently on its new brass hinge
is how she came into my life, a wing, the kind of beginning
I could never foretell nor dream, can't fully recall.
She was all whiteness, a glimmer of nothing
surrounded by light in a spell of white blossom –
chaste tree; no, smaller – so small even the air
had to inhale itself to see her, to make room
for her arrival. Then, all day our heads were moons
inside the house, one moon alongside the other
as though we were thinking only of snow.
We had nothing but air and hands and limbs,
and the shape of things we couldn't understand
and probably never will. We sat on chairs
for a long time, until moonlight flooded the room
and our breath sank so low we could have been
birch trees instead or slippery fish, flounders,
flickers of silver in a world so vast
even our bodies lost themselves, salt in water.
Think about this differently: there are no ends
and no beginnings and even in dreams
the one who enters is only half there
in a loose dress, getting ready to dance
or to die with hands held out, a supplication
to something ordinary, the starlight, the sky.
We may have been meant but we may not.
Years now, and we have held each other
like all animals hold and we have learnt
to come back at high tide or when the wind

blows out our eyes, to come back in
to the table and upright chairs
in case we've forgotten the length of life,
one face beside another, pupil, iris, lid.
I've lived through her white lily, her hawthorn
like a small bird might, noticing, alighting,
and I can say nothing about love
beyond the plates and bowls we ate from,
year after year, our cutlery leaving ghost lines
on the crock, our lips on stained cups.
Here is her arm and here the horizon,
held level for however long it can.
Think differently about this:
there are some things we just can't change;
the years, and how we've drifted
from room to room and far out
on to hills and fields and beaches
where the whales roll in without meaning
to, where the place for leaving is made clear
by birds' bones and grey seals
who slide from air to water
as though the sea were an open door.

Oars

I cross the sand bare-foot
to my man and his small row-boat.

The sea shocks my feet as he hands me a jacket
and together we push out and climb in.

On the water everything is colder
and stray bits of kelp nuzzle at the boat.

We find the sheltered bay
and wait all morning for fish.

Come on, you row a bit, he says,
diesel engine for a throat.

I row and row out to nowhere,
to the deep grey

that keeps changing places with itself.

The Seal King

He's caught nothing but small fry,
silver flicks on the smeared white deck –
ghost-fish, she'll say,
barely worth the smoke.

The boat has no need for the shore –
one edge defines the other
well enough out here:
salt-body, sleek bow-ribs,
keel of heartwood.

It's all lines:
the long lull of the water
and the ache where the sun hits –
light beam a fillet blade.

He takes the tackle in,
hauls anchor,
reels the blue whale weight of it,
left over right
as the chain coils
in the boat at his feet.

But it doesn't come up alone.

A seal comes,
pebble-smooth, rock-grey,
mottled with pale lichen,
skin of an aspen,
girth of a tree, he'll say.

Enough to feed the winter,
to stave the cold if he kills it,
if his knife will dig deep enough,
if the blubber will part
to the point where the blood floods the brain
and the eyes clot with the slow glug of it.
If his arm is strong enough to strike the right blow
and the boat stays steady
and the water waits,

lapping,
boat like an eye, watching.

The seal two fathoms down
with his knife.

So late, she'll say, as the boat comes in,
cast-iron pan in her small rough hand.

King of all seals, he'll say,
and she'll press his face with her palm.

Brown Bear Walt Whitman

Oh fish I eat you! Oh berries I eat you! Sex nipples on bushes and fish so quicksilver, they flick through the water like shooting-stars. I eat them ravenously. I am of berries. Also, I am of fish. I hunker in the water to catch miraculous dinner! My paws are tremendous! My belly is tremendous with hunger, a shipping container with no cargo, a night sky with no moon. When the hunger is here, fish are goners! Berries are goners! I splosh the length of the river for the best harvest. The water chases me timelessly. Sometimes filth comes downriver. I keep eating because I do, I must, and I keep loving the eating. Watch the strange fish jump! Watch the berries twerk in the wind!

Midsummer

After Tranströmer

An orange light
streams off my skin.
Midsummer.
Brass tubas of heat.
I close my eyes.
There is a buzzing world.
There is a cave
where the living swim
in clear pools.

Waiting to Water the Ponies

It must be summer.
The man is naked on the path,
early fog wrapping his quiet skin
in its loose, grainy light.

His hands are full –
a bag of apples; an orange bucket
with *Fire* written on it –
and he's saying something,
sound carrying across the field
to the ponies with uncut manes
and tails thick with mud and rain.

Their summer blood brings them
one by one out of nothing,
to the blank man and his bright bucket
in the small corridor between them and us.

They take it in turns to drink
the fire-water and eat the soft red apples
the man has saved.

The Bell

When I put on my shoes
a bell starts clanging and doesn't stop
until I reach the flooded October fields beyond the river.
It's true rainwater and river-water boast over the back roads.
There's no knowing when it will end.
Not this Sunday, not yet.

At the field edges,
a couple of floating Friesians
split from the herd.
The whites of my eyes bloat with them.
My shoes are silent like fruit.

Riparian Zone

In July and August 2010 monsoon rains flooded the Indus River in Pakistan and breached two major dams in Sindh Province. 20 million people were affected.

Take the bucket at the tent's door.
Ignore the flies, their constant sucking
and walk like you know
why you're going to the river.
It's August and everything is swollen.
Through the torn sheet I watch you,
sunlight erasing your head.
You swing the bucket like the hand of a friend.
For now, there is no dust.
You duck beneath trees, a row of babul and sheesham.
At the water's edge, you bend to the flood.
The river is browner than usual and big.

Opening Up the Back Field

It's quiet with the fence gone.

John rolls up the barbed-wire,
stacks the posts, a huddle of femurs, by the shed.

In the holes, air and mud,
the *slub* of west coast rain.

The whole world's doubled
with the fence down,

as though one reel of barbed-wire can change
not just the way the field looks.

John says *Aye* but he never comes over again.
Slub goes the mud.
Slub goes the rain.

Coming of Age

for F

When the light finally comes,
a single ray at the curtain's edge,

the girl moves over
and takes it in her hand.

She listens to it crackle, the soft split
of the sun-pulse, the open ache.

She wraps the light carefully
in the deep folds of her bed,

climbs in after it,
glows.

A Silent Film for All Ages

we eat the first true leaves as the light pools into the woods

we know how to skin rabbits but there are none
only stripped brambles and kicked earth where they might have been

by day we look for birds – long hours with craned necks

we speak about berries and the colour of the sky
red ones are dangerous but white equally so

where the beech trees end there's a clearing with a fair

deep tyre-marks in the turf
red and white stalls with candy-floss and Yogi Bear

hope has two hooks – one in our bellies and one other

we don't cry or whoop but we ride every ride
and fill our pockets with prizes – key-fobs, notebooks, miniature
plastic toys

when it's finally time to go we make wishes in the half-light

in our dreams we rewind everything

In Esther's Garden

for Ed

Every strawberry is blood and muscle,
small as a swallow's heart
with pip eyes on the outside of the fruit.

We eat at least two thousand, whole flocks,
and then put handmade mush
into slippery, unflappable pots.

Our laughter migrates all the way
to France, to Africa, and arrives back
dismayed somehow, thinner.

With mush-arms and mush-hands,
we go inside for spoons, scoop
sticky flesh from our freckled skin.

These are our wings! Esther says,
doing a snow-angel on the lino;
or something like that – it's such a long time ago.

And Did You Get What You Wanted from This Life, Even So?*

'Horses!' she says, straight out like that.
'Horses and hills and some kind of small, portable fire that never goes out.'
I look at her side-on. Her nose is big;
she has lips that are smaller than mine, pursed and chapped.
'Is that it?' I ask, half joking.
Her eyes are grey; she has hair like sand eels and a blue felt hat.

Taken from Raymond Carver's poem, 'Late Fragment'.

For We Are Not Horses

I'm walking with Papa Buddha on the new lane that leads
like an eager dog to the horses. It's Sunday and the sun is so hot

Buddha's white house is a blur and my shoes ooze on the new tar.
Bringing up the rear, my mother in a green silk jacket like a sun spurge.

In less than a mile, the good, brown horses, muzzles down, sweep-tugging
the grass as though they're embroidering the field. Buddha's pipe is smoking.

I lean into him as we lean against the gate, watch their easy slickness.
What I like about them most is their loaf-tin faces and their out-breath huff

when I tell them I love them. It doesn't take a genius to know my mother
wants to be a horse – long legs, glossy mane. But we all know she's not.

The whole verge is aglow with dandelions and I pick a bunch, hold it out,
but Buddha laughs and the horses snort as the milk drips from the stalks

in nasty sticky globs. When we walk back, we walk back slowly,
my mother up front with her tail swishing.

Big Davie

After he got out of prison, Big Davie loved horses. He worked with them all winter on someone else's land. Brown horses and black horses and some with manes that covered their eyes. It was a long winter and the rain came and never went, like a baby's first cry. It nudged at the stable doors and overflowed the tin roofs. It dripped off the end of Big Davie's nose. In the spring one of them died in his stall, a stallion so big the men couldn't lift him, with a black coat and jelly eyes. When the vet came, Big Davie had to cut him and the blood pooled and the rain swilled salty. He eased the meat out.

Adumbrate

An umbrella with an alarm so you remember when it's raining.

The abundance of lumbago in Humberside.

A human muffled by autumn leaves or snowdrifts or bedding.

A man with a Daimler admitting a 3-point turn on a one-way street.

A scatter bomb detonated at midsummer.

A humungous brown cloud blotting out the uneducated estates.

Umbilical attachment to not knowing what's going to happen but
administering as if you do.

The remains of a broken, silent cerebellum.

The state of being mummified.

A wound wide open.

A damp underpass where dogs drown, where the river's monumental,

where every year of Our Lord is a year of shadow.

The Woodchester Beast

Sundown and the men have been waiting all day for the news,
drinking pints of ale in the Hare & Hounds,
lisping about the big cat, her broad head,
her teeth and claws.

Somewhere in the soft woods,
deep in the purple fuzz of trees and brambles,
the big cat is prowling, each paw
the size of a human face.

Nobody has seen her by day, but as light
dims and the birds murmur to roost,
experts report sightings of a shadowy figure
in and out of the tree-line, something
loping with intent, biding time at the body
of water near Nailsworth Common,
before slipping into the absolute
black of binocular cases and lens caps.

When they found her, she was ripped at the belly,
guts torn out in one swift manoeuvre,
head mangled.

I Took God with Me to the Prison

After Kerry Hardie

I took God with me to the prison. I said, 'Look, there's Ben and Lewis. There's Brian and Mark. They've been here a while. They've got matching sweatshirts. Their faces are hatching things… This is the length of a corridor and these are the walls, bricks painted white, cement painted white even though everyone knows it's the colour of dead teeth, the colour of the space where dreams used to be… See that man over there and that woman, with belts big enough to hold the world up – they're the keys. They're more awake when the keys jangle, more awake when the keys slot into the locks and the metal rattle-clanks against metal. They're more awake when the keys fit and the keys turn and the keys jostle in their pockets like animal bones… That light up there, that's artificial. That ground is just a cover, a false statement hiding real earth.' I asked God to look outside and pointed out the barbed wire fence, the perimeter walls beyond perimeter walls. 'Outside there's sky,' I said, 'If you crane your neck far enough back.' God looked at the sky – bright blue (it was a clear day) – and looked at me and said nothing…' Some of the men are here for a reason. Some of the men have done things other men don't do. Come through here and I'll show you their artwork. I'll show you pencils and pens, the squashed tubes of paint, the poems they write. Look, here's a picture of sunlight and a woman sitting…And this is where scissors are locked and pallet knives and staple guns. This is where fingers slip…' I don't know why but I showed God the toilets, one for staff, one for prisoners. In the staff toilet there's a Gauguin poster from the time he spent in Tahiti. The women in the painting are sitting in a forest, surrounded by lush vegetation. All those leaves and trees and flowers.

The Swim

Now for the other life. The one without mistakes
　　　　　　　—Lou Lipsitz

I'm awake. I'm walking downstairs to the kitchen.
The light is long, a slippery white eel through the curtain.

Remember that night we camped by the lake
and there were bears outside? That's what it's like now –

heart racing like a skimmed pebble, palms sweating.
Each new breath, a pike bone.

There's nowhere else in the poem to go.
I'm stuck at the kitchen door.

It's possible a year passes, maybe more,
enough time for my husband to drift in,

for me to stare after him and shout
at the top of my voice, mouth like a reef.

'Don't light the gas! Whatever you do, don't light the gas!'
But he lights the gas and the kitchen explodes in an aurora of light and heat.

Soon the whole house is ablaze, all the bedrooms, all the roof beams.
Everything we own is burnt in a white heat, like a mirage.

Then I swim out of the poem into nothing.

O

in Memoriam P

You have only one lung
and a tube to outside air, an open gill.
Your body is cut up like this, like that.
And every time you breathe
a bird sings a terrible song,
It won't be long, it won't be long.

Opiliones

Last chance to see the harvestman.

The spider has superfine pins for legs,
thin glinting things
that catch the occasional light.

Strictly speaking, this is not a spider
but you crush it anyway,
watch it pull its pins to its ball-bearing body

like a trap springing in slow motion.

Blackbird

If the human race fails to survive all this, it will be because it can't get interested in its own annihilation. —Ted Hughes in a letter to Terry Gifford, 1993

I'll find the blackbird hiding in the ivy.
Its orange beak will give it away,
its orange-rimmed eye
like the bromide ring around the moon.
I'll see its machinery – the plumed wings, the precision-tool beak –
and I'll crush it between my palms,
feel the nice urgent pumping,
the scratchy lizard legs.

It'll not be enough
so I'll find a stone, any old stone.

I'll wedge the bird by its shivering wings
and smash it in one fell swoop,
its egg-sized cranium,
the stream-lined bony font of its breast.

There'll be no heart,
no lungs full of upper air,
only the smashing spurt of blood
and ribs like pins – the bird's own cage.

Doing Bird

for the incarcerated

You hear nothing, not even the unseasonal rain.
Flinch-brains like flick-knives fighting the rain.

You have tight bodies, mouths like beaks.
I show you white feathers, wet with rain.

You're here longer than me, you know more,
but knowing's a loose thread, the silver of rain.

You're wing-men and claw-men, faces like cliffs
where you hunker and squawk in the crumbling rain.

You know carelessness like you know love,
a popped eye, a broken lip, hopeless in the pouring rain.

And in your palms, reversed love, others' blood,
homeless pain. You wrestle with the indifference of rain.

On Fridays you watch me and call out my name.
Your stories unwing me. I walk home in the rain.

Hare

In Memoriam Jyoti Singh

I'm carrying the hare along the road. One of its back legs is hanging by a single tendon, blood seeping slowly in the cold. It's early morning, but the hare is late. The school bus has taken it by surprise, for the last time. I'm holding it like a newborn baby, one hand beneath its head, the other beneath its backside. It's heavy. It weighs roughly as much as a fully grown, well-fed tomcat. It's the kind of weight I'd prefer to sling over my shoulder.

For some time now, I've been unable to let the images go: the bus in the semi-dark, the young woman and her male friend; the blood on the men's hands and all their wide eyes in the confines of the vehicle; the metal air; the woman's voice which I can hear, again and again, no matter where I look.

The body is still warm and limp, still supple, and I keep half-expecting its eyes to blink, its legs to jerk awake. I half-expect the hare to jump and charge away from me. But it doesn't. I carry it into the woods and put it down beneath a rhododendron bush. I lay it out in such a way that the gashed leg is invisible and it looks, it really looks, as though the hare is wide alive and running. It doesn't matter whether I'm doing this for me or for all hares.

I find a few branches and twigs and make a kind of woody tent over the body. I don't do this for other roadkill, but I've been watching the hares all year – there's a pair. Or there was. They circle the house like sentinels, beginning on the eastern side with the sun and working their way round through the orchard, past the hen-run and into the woods. I watch them through the windows, their black-tipped ears, their long, powerful hind-legs that work like suspension coils, easing the body up and forward, down and forward, perpetually sprung; ready, I supposed, for the unexpected.

By now it's a familiar story. The woman with a young, smiling face and soft skin. Her softness in the last light of the evening. All the shouting men, their mouths, their drenched clothes.

It's a small back road with little traffic, but the school bus passes twice a day and the driver doesn't mean to hit it. He's late and the kids are waiting, out in the cold on a corner of turf.

I stroke its long ears back against its head, stroke its fine coat, white belly, small face. Hares have kinetic skulls – they're jointed – which allows for a degree of movement between the front and back sections. It helps absorb the force of impact as the hare strikes the ground.

The iron bar. The shadow faces. The quiet glistening of the steering wheel, an empty glass bottle, an eye.

Swan

When the year turns she flies in,
lily white amongst the river reeds

and the boys knew to stay away,
her power neck, her mute beak.

The women pace the shore
from first light, feet like eyes,

but it's dusk before they find them,
clothes torn, skin in tatters,

faces peeled like apples.
The mother only knows them by their hands.

When the Hunger is Here and the Anger

When the hunger is here and the anger,
the horses lift their muzzles and snort
in the manner of horses, truthfully,
with a mane-flicking, hoof-stomping truth
that sticks to the roof of your mouth
as you watch from the edge of the field,
floodwater lapping a hollow
where the grass slowly sinks;
as though the water were the night drawing down
or the closing curtains of a time
when fine brown horses canter
to the edge of the fabric,
waiting for you to find your voice and raise it,
waiting for you to take the reins
when the hunger is here and the anger.

When the hunger is here and the anger,
you remember the rich man
who starved his horses,
how they died painfully, slowly,
over weeks of neglect and mistreatment,
how their ribs stopped their skin
from sinking deeper,
how their eyes stopped breathing on the final day
– brown beadlet anemones with no sea –
how he never knew the coarse brown coat of the mare
nor the way the stallion hoofed the fence to be with her,
knowing the only way to live is with others,
whether they're hurting or dancing or dying,

no matter how hard it rains or how deep the fields fill
when the hunger is here and the anger.

When the hunger is here and the anger,
there's no room for the necessity of grief
and the small bird of the body
stabs its beak into the day again and again,
like a robot working a conveyor belt;
and all sense of faith is lost in an endless flight
from the soft feathers of the self,
from the bird's precise, miraculous migration
from one timeless, embodied life to another,
covering thousands of miles without stopping
to look back, without suffering the hooks of doubt or lack,
as though the path is clear for every small bird, every swallow
and bunting, every finch who lands at the new lake
and drinks the brown floodwater gratefully, with relief,
when the hunger is here and the anger.

When the hunger is here and the anger
and the path is littered with clear-fell and bombed homes
and burnt-out faces of people broken
in the way the racehorse is broken,
hurdle after hurdle,
sweat steaming off it like a ghost-horse,
one after the other withering into a grey sky,
all of us racehorses with anemone eyes,
stinging and seeking
with blind hands and blind feet –
then you know that the song the small birds sing
is the one you belong to,
the song you and everyone else

can bring into the long dark days
when the hunger is here and the anger.

A Poem Before Breakfast

before the door opens and the pony crashes in with hoof-dirt and flicky muzzle. You ordered eggs and toast but Pony's got the order wrong. You don't feel like complaining, so you take the chomped grass and lay out its clumpy wet mass on the desk. There's clover in there, but you don't feel lucky. You say, *Thank you, Pony. I love your ragged mane and old crock teeth*. And you take your time with the grass breakfast. You think, in hard times you might have to eat grass and clover. There may be a time for learning how to graze, to pluck sweet halms from the fields and work them with green teeth; to be a cud-chewer, adept at regurgitation and infinitely patient with the slowness of cellulose. You might become a ruminant at last on the empty, philosophical hills.

Woodpigeon

In the distance, my soul is not satisfied
—Pablo Neruda

To skulk at dusk at the tree-line.
To know restlessness better than anyone.
To waddle beneath the Scots pine.
To not enter the clearing.
To not think about tomorrow. To not remember.
To make no sound. To hoard sound in your roundness.
To apprehend grey, its shiftiness.
To be hesitant.
To not give up. To be infinitive.
To be open and to move towards openness.

Gardener

for D

This is the gardener I was talking about last year,
the one with short trousers and a trowel with a blue wooden handle,
loose in his hand like a smoking gun, only not.

He's more relaxed than me, somehow warmer,
and his slow walk reminds me of the way I always wanted to be
but never could, the way we all might want some day.

He is solid in his arms and legs, like an ox, only not.
A small, not-asking-for-much ox who stretches over the beds
like a muscled eel would

or a man who knows about growth and soil.
He's an ox and an eel at the same time –
something to be proud of. I'd tell him if I could.

Should we go over and say hello, tell him he's a fine man,
that he reminds us of things we never normally speak of?
I say yes but you say no –

it's too in-your-face
and the man might out-blush his sweet peas or out-swell his pumpkin.
Let's keep him there as he is:

a quiet doer on the brown earth,
raking in the evening as though each crumb of soil
is a newborn coming into air.

The Visitation

After Stanley Spencer's 1912-13 painting

The woman will arrive at any time of day
and place her feet on the threshold.

The door will either hang, squeaking and invisible
on its broad, expansive hinges,

or float off into the village
as a funeral raft for the next door neighbour's child:

they'll push him out on the river
with a bunch of vervain and a pipe.

All the children will cry
and afterwards the world will be lighter
and glow a little orange in the evening.

When the woman enters
she'll see each careful item,

a silver pot with a bone handle,
tea diffusing like blood in water.

There are no men here
only their kicking inside.

Come in. Sit down. Listen.

The woman has things to say
that will set the birds singing.

She cannot stay too long,
cannot outstay anything –

the dresser in the kitchen
will always persist for longer,

wood rich with sweating decades,
with the salt and the blood of the air.

The walls contain themselves,
so too the cupboards, the cups,

those tiny vessels, their china chink
like thrushes crushing snails on stones.

The First Swallow of Summer

The tilt of the wing
through the open window.
Light streams in,
ribbons of it draping the floor,
the old machinery, a carcass hook
that doubles up as perch.

Man of the Machars, Whithorn Peninsula

Black nettles cringe at his gate,
old home harled with birdshit.

Wind and the torpor of rust
unhinge time, string it out

between roof beam and local hill,
where the long black horizon

seems to underline the need
to ask questions: is this a man

with eyes that raise moths from the road,
part carrion crow, part stone?

Drumlins

Whatever glacier decided to mould the mud and rock like this
must have been inspired by knowing
that you can't stop what's coming.
You can't roll back the turf and level the moraine.
You can't call an ancient hummock an epiglottis
hanging in the larynx between now and then.

Tog Muhoni

Because when you see him you know, small light in a night forest,
that his name is Tog Muhoni and his smile tells the way the river bends
and how he crossed it, one foot dragging behind like a snapped limb:
to stay or to go? You're late for something, driving, and your whole life
is mapped out in the arm he's missing. The shoulder blade is intact,
you can see as you slow down, rub the breath from the windscreen
and stare in a way your mother would have scolded. An owl
inside your head this morning, eyes, silent inquisition:
his body seems to shift, migrate from one shape to another
or he's just a ghost waving in the cold, winter air wafting.
All those times you stood outside and watched your breath
cloud, large animal, moon face, hoof-less. You know his days
go deeper. Snow hole with a man curled in it. Small pack
stitched of deerskin. A fine knife, furs.

Instead of turning right, you stop the car and wait. Something in you:
a shiny, dark-skinned kernel, a need you've put away
like a button from your dead father's coat, a need for history
or flight. No, both. Where you're going, you don't know
but everything you thought was true is false, everything
you've learnt flows out like guts from a split belly,
the strings of intestine you can read your fortune in,
your fate. But you can't look forwards, only back
at the black hulk of the car as you walk off or through
or out. Where are you now? Wait.

The street is unfamiliar; you've never walked here before,
never walked like this with your whole face seeing,
eyes, yes, but also lips, nose, skin, and the skin's soft,

barely visible vellus that marks you out as animal or bird,
a small hawk maybe, all seeing. You can't be sure
but the figure walking over seems to be singing,
mouth wide like a warm dark stone and then the song
coming close, as though the singer's inside you -
you're the lone singer! Be still a while and listen.
Wide streets, wider than you imagined possible,
car-less now, each building flanking something beyond
the mind's eye, something flickering inside an opening.
Never too late. A soul. Small black purse.

When he steps up you know his name is Tog Muhoni
and his life is a fire you forgot to feed, a time you forgot
to live. You drape your sorrow around yourself
but he laughs and with his one good arm
lifts your chin to the sky like a mother might
tilt her child. Somewhere in the other town
your desk is waiting with its papers and books,
a lamp leaning in like an eye piercing the same space
over and over. Tog Muhoni looks at you
as though you've never known looking before.
A blue shawl of looking. An embrace.

Felt Sense

Tongue hanging out, incisors like flick-knives,
she shoots up the track to the stirk field,
where you lose her.

Slow arrival of rain,
felt sense tapping your head
as you straddle the barbed-wire fence.

Gut in her eye, stench of blood at the heart of her
and all the spilling from the roe deer,
steaming organs in the half-light.

Licking her wounds,
the dog leaves her bright, half dead:

you have to boot the life out
in the brash of the field.

Stone

I

The nights are the hardest.
It's the time of year, the harsh wind.
But the truth is
the horses have left; they're not lost.

'Excuse me, I've lost two horses.
One's grey with pit-black eyes
and the other's called Nightbird.
Have you seen them?'

Her yard is awash with the wind – rolling buckets
and bits of plastic flicking in the gloom.
She's standing there in old black boots
and trousers two sizes too big for her.
She's familiar, but I don't know how.

'Neither seen nor heard,' she smiles.

But she knows what horses look like.
She knows they have strong legs and tails,
that they cross fields we can't see,
from one white world to another,
somewhere warmer, somewhere brighter.

I'm waiting in the cold with a straight back
and broad shoulders, trying to hold the place up;
to slow things down and bring something back,
not just my horses.

'You'll not find them here,' she says,
'And the wind's colossal tonight.'

Her house is shivering and cracking,
halfway between human and shack.

She beckons me in out of the blaring wind:
firelight polishing the hearth;
dogs with thicker coats than mine,
shaggy black wire for hair, faces like hers.

'The horses will be there in the morning,' she says,
but I've already turned to go.

I thank her,
tell her I'm taking the path east.

II

Father's ten years cold in the ground: lungs gave out.
He spent his days digging up stone,
lugging it about from one place to another
for someone else to pound in with a truck,
load it, deliver it.

In the end, he was just skin and bone,
a leather skeleton working the hill.

He used to joke about digging his own grave,
over and over, as though the whole hill scooped out
wouldn't be enough to home him.

Stone to build flats and factories,
or broken into smaller bits for roads
or harling for bungalows.

It was the stone that got him down –
dust motes in his lungs
like a murmuration of starlings.

When he didn't come home
I chopped wood and lit a fire.

On the mantle was a small ivory horse
with one eye missing and a wire tail.
I called it Captain because it didn't belong to me;
it was foreign.
It must have come from some old, exotic place
where everything's intricately carved from ivory –
knives, forks, spoons, plates, even the beds,

all carved from the cold, creamy stuff.
Everything would be polished and gleaming.

One animal's tusk made into the shape of a horse.
I always thought it would weigh more.

Dusk came and went and there was no father,
no change to the contour of the lane.

I peeled potatoes at the kitchen sink
but the knife was too big for my hands
and it slipped.
I slipped.

The next thing I know,
I'm in a land where there's nothing but trees.
I rub my eyes and blink
but it's real and there's snow on the ground;
there's no blood and I'm standing
with a stone in my fist.

The air's hard, sharp,
and all around are radial pine,
row upon row in an endless deep green world.
No clouds, no birds.

The place is silent; it's like an inverse desert
with trees instead of sand.
It doesn't matter which row I follow,
I meet only pine.
The smell is astringent, clean.

I walk for some time on one path
but my body's like a puppet,
half asleep and baggy
and my hand hurts
and I can't feel my feet.

I walk and breathe,
listening to the thud of my heart
beneath skin and thin flesh,
within a frail cage of ribs;
heart half the size of a horse's,
real or ivory.

For a long time, I'm afraid.
I can't say where I am
or whether it will some day end.

All I know is,
the stone came unbidden.

III

I don't remember so well anymore.
My mind's less able, less sure
that what I've chosen is the right choice:
to live in a place where there are more animals than men.

It's a kind of prayer to the earth,
no matter how strange that sounds.

I try not to measure or judge,
just to keep going and care for the horses,
find enough food, be prepared for the nights.

The long, cold nights begin in May or June
and seem to go on forever
though there are no years anymore,
there are no seasons.
In February I've seen hawthorn flower
and fruit swell
and swallows come.

It's hard to tell,
but the horses left in June, I think.
We were living in a ruin
at the foot of a hill where nobody goes –
it's boggy ground and it rains a lot.
A river flows to the south.

After I fixed the roof and repaired the walls –
I'm good with my hands –
it was shelter enough
for me and the horses.

It isn't our land but it feels right;
it's all we need;
it stood up to the nights for a long time.

No windows, just a door
and a hole in the roof
for a makeshift chimney;
dry bracken on a packed earth floor.

Not what most humans prefer,
but comfortable enough
and if you spend all day outside,
the dark is less risky.

I keep clean in nearby streams
(the river's ferocious),
and forage whatever food I can –
nuts and berries, leaves and roots.

I see more deer than before,
whole tides of them flooding the hills,
upsetting the scree.
I could kill them easily.

Two horses, big ones,
with strong legs and long tails.
They might be ancient wild horses
or pedigrees left over from a breeder.
There's no way of knowing.

They appeared one wet day,
one male, one female,

and I gave them names,
took them in.

I didn't care where they came from
or how cold the nights got
as long as the horses were there.

I can smell them – that deep, musty, tangy,
sometimes sweet, sometimes grassy smell –
and I can see them moving away from here.

It's the stone's fault.

I can watch horses for days,
how they tread the ground,
how their haunches twitch
with flies as they graze.
I follow the line of the jaw
as it curves into the cheek muscle,
joins the neck like the f-hole in a fiddle,
like the furl of a fern.

These are difficult times.

IV

I'm laying bracken over the shit and mud
where the horses and I bed down.
It's slow work because I make it so:
I want every ounce of life,
no matter how tough.

And then, out of nowhere, she arrives.

The horses start.
Nightbird canters past her to the woods
and the other follows,
as though they're indivisible.

It's a sunny day and she's near enough
to shout a greeting.
I pretend to complete my task,
pulling the dry fronds,
but it's my wits I'm gathering.

'Hello,' she says, half-smiling, bold.
She has a pair of black boots
and trousers two sizes too big for her.

'I don't have food. It's just me and the horses.'

I want to walk past her but I can't.
I stand there, glaring.

'I've brought you something,' she says,
putting her hand in her pocket
and holding the thing out.

'Here,' she jerks the gift, 'take it.'

'It's just me and the horses,' I plead,
as if she'd not heard.

The gift is hidden in a rag
and weighs more than I thought.
I put it in my pocket
and try to forget it.
But it hangs there like a third bollock,
only heavier,
and as I begin to lift more bracken,
it knocks against my thigh.

I've turned my back to dismiss her
but it's a mistake,
as so much is.

'It's from your father,' she lies.

V

It's the smoothest oval stone I've ever seen,
and sits perfect in my palm like a plum.
I turn it over,
relish its surface,
try to unpack its minerals,
but I can't.
A kind of granite? Feldspar?
The stone stares back.

What order these things go in,
I don't know,
but once the stone was here,
the horses stayed away all night,
sometimes all the following day,
as though they didn't like the smell of me,
as though something wasn't right.

Lift off my scalp
and there's the stone,
cooried like an egg
in its fine, warm nest.

The nights are the hardest.
It's the time of year, the harsh wind.

Acknowledgements

Some of these poems, or earlier versions of them, were published in *The Glasgow Herald, New Writing Scotland, Poetry Scotland, Causeway/Cabhsair, Earthlines, Entanglements: New Ecopoetry, Swamp, Dark Mountain, Southlight, Ecozon@, New Writing Dundee, Glasgow Review of Books, Fourfold,* and *Templar Anthology 2015.*

'Bird-Woman' was highly commended in the Wigtown Poetry Competition (2013) and was included in the *The Forward Book of Poetry 2017* (London: Forward Worldwide, 2016). 'Doing Bird' was short-listed in the Bridport Poetry Prize (2014). 'Stone' was published in pamphlet form by Atlantic Press in March 2016, together with illustrations by artist, Mat Osmond. Mat's work can be found at www.strandlinebooks.co.uk

I'd like to thank Elizabeth Reeder, David Borthwick, Jen Hadfield and John Burnside for their generous support and encouragement. I am especially grateful to Kath Burlinson, Paul Oertel and Nancy Spanier, who entered my life at exactly the right moment. I am also greatly indebted to the Scottish Book Trust for their continual help, guidance and the New Writer Award 2014, without which this collection would have taken even longer to write.

I'd also like to thank Tamsin Haggis and Rachel Connor for being there, for chats about creative process and essential cups of endless tea. Thanks also to artist, Kate Walters, for 'The Bird my Brother', the book's cover image. Kate's work can be found at http://www.katewalters.co.uk. To all the wonderful women who have buoyed me up along the way – Deborah Andrews, Becks Denny, Dorothy Alexander, Defne Çizakça – thank you! And last but by no means least, thanks to my husband and my daughters for The Love.

Lightning Source UK Ltd.
Milton Keynes UK
UKHW041230140119
335543UK00001B/265/P